The Little White Wolf

LEE ALLEN

© 2023 Lee Allen. All rights reserved.

*No part of this book may be reproduced, stored in a retrieval system,
or transmitted by any means without the written permission of the author.
Published by Lee Allen*

ISBN Paperback: 978-1-952648-98-4
ISBN Hardcover: 978-1-952648-99-1
ISBN Ebook: 978-1-952648-97-7

Library of Congress Control Number: 2018909182

*Any people depicted in stock imagery provided by Getty Images are models,
and such images are being used for illustrative purposes only.
Certain stock imagery © Getty Images.*

*This is a work of fiction. All of the characters, names, incidents, organizations, and dialogue in this
novel are either the products of the author's imagination or are used fictitiously.*

*Because of the dynamic nature of the Internet, any web addresses or links contained in this book may have changed
since publication and may no longer be valid. The views expressed in this work are solely those of the author and
do not necessarily reflect the views of the publisher, and the publisher hereby disclaims any responsibility for them*

I dedicate this book to my lovely wife, Susan, without whose patience, love, and hard work it never would have been completed.

In the early spring, the she-wolf, Sara, had her pups. Naturally, she had told Jared, the father, in no uncertain terms to stay out of the den till further notice. She did expect the otherwise banished father to bring food regularly for herself and the babies.

Sara and Jared had seven strong, healthy pups in various shades of black, gray, and brown. They named the four females Temp, Bard, Eele, and Suni. The three males were Harro, Kayle, and Tomor. And then there was the eighth tiny wolf—the runt, Leesu, the only one with a white coat.

From the beginning, Leesu was only half as big as his brothers and sisters, and his mother feared he would not survive. As the days of spring marched into summer, he grew a little and seemed to thrive in the sunshine and open air.

The other members of the pack wished to destroy the pup because he was different and they saw him as a threat. But Jared would not allow his smallest pup to be destroyed till Leesu had a chance to contribute to the pack

As was his duty, Jared took the pups out to hunt and learn the skills they would need to survive in the wild. The pups learned to hide in the grass so still that they could jump a passing rabbit. But no matter how still he lay, Leesu's coat always gave him away, and he returned to the den with an empty stomach. He tried to wade into the stream with his siblings to fish, but his legs were so short that he fell in every hole, coming up soaked with no fish. His brothers and sisters laughed at him. Again the others in the pack pointed out that Jared and Sara couldn't take care of the little white pup forever. He would have to learn to survive on his own or die.

Leesu knew the pack was watching him, so he tried even harder to fit in. He was very fast and learned he could run faster than his bigger siblings. He knew he could run down those rabbits and mice if only he could get a little jump on them. But because his white coat shone brightly against the dark forest, the animals always saw him coming. He even thought that because he was so small, he might learn to climb a tree to nab a bird or some eggs. He soon learned that not even very small wolves have paws and claws meant for climbing trees

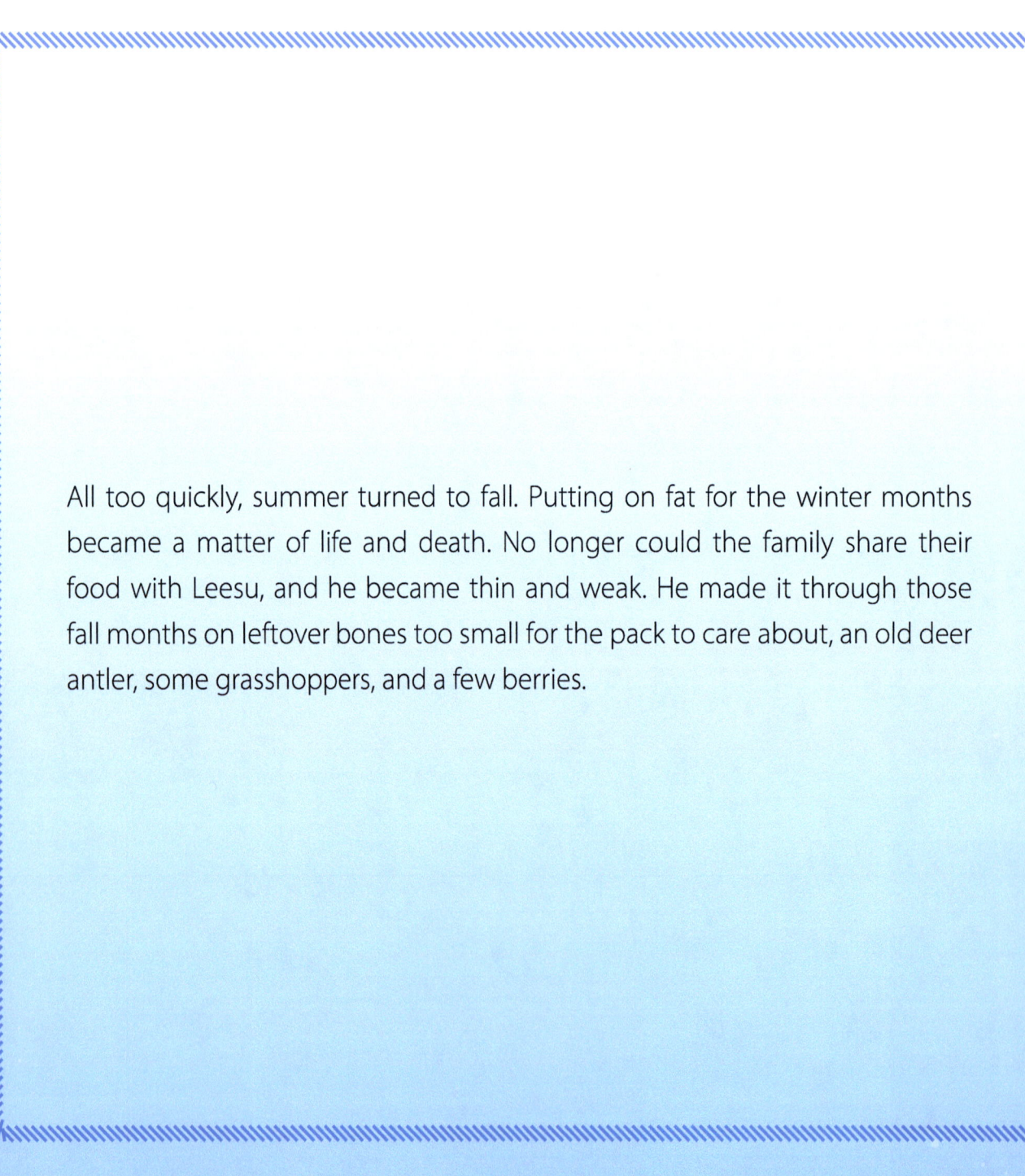

All too quickly, summer turned to fall. Putting on fat for the winter months became a matter of life and death. No longer could the family share their food with Leesu, and he became thin and weak. He made it through those fall months on leftover bones too small for the pack to care about, an old deer antler, some grasshoppers, and a few berries.

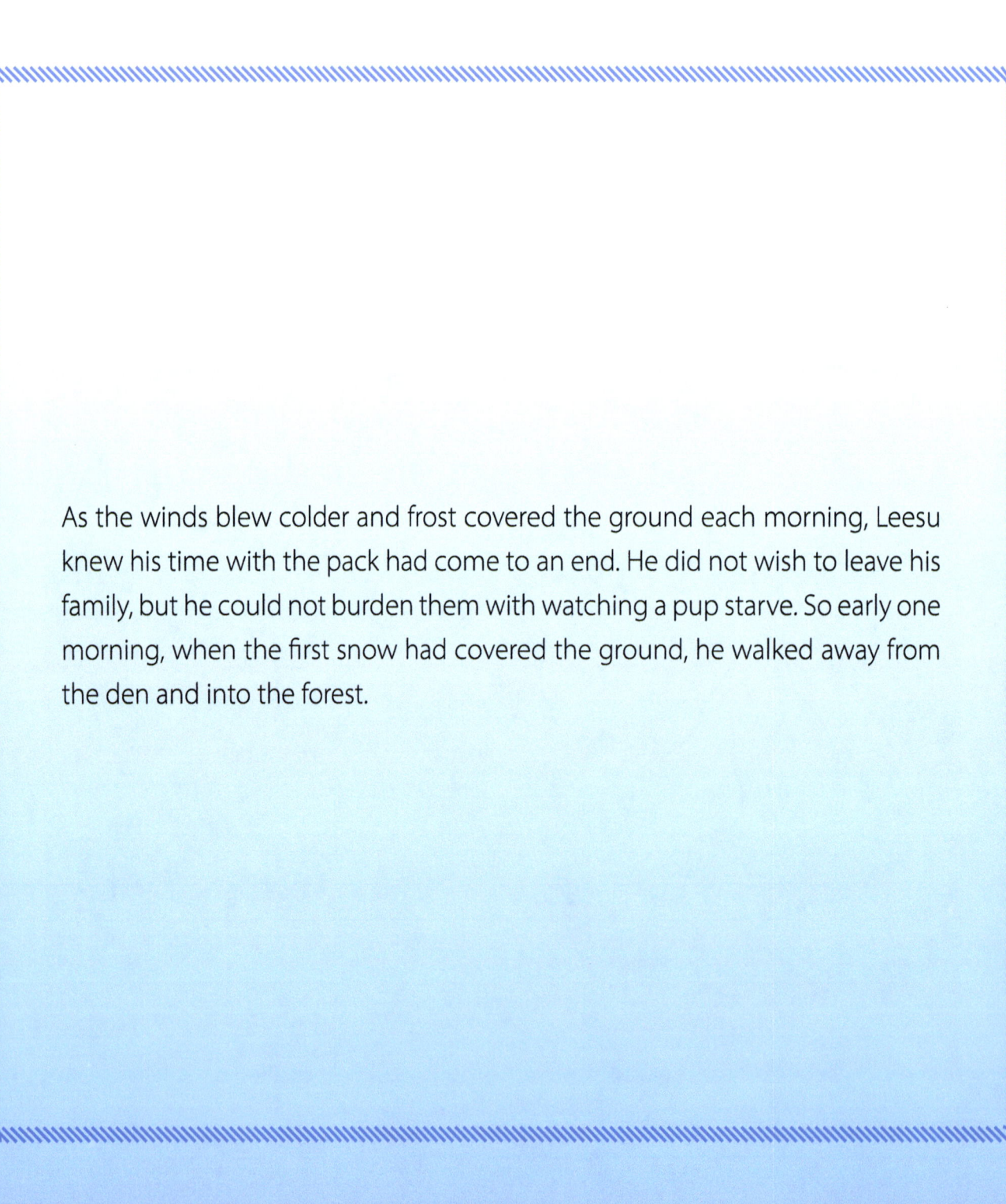

As the winds blew colder and frost covered the ground each morning, Leesu knew his time with the pack had come to an end. He did not wish to leave his family, but he could not burden them with watching a pup starve. So early one morning, when the first snow had covered the ground, he walked away from the den and into the forest.

Leesu was so weak from hunger that several hours later he collapsed in the snow at the edge of a forest clearing. He was so tired that he could barely keep his eyes open. Suddenly, a movement to his left caught his eye. It was a rabbit moving into the clearing directly in front of him. Though he knew the rabbit would spot him, as they always did, he lay perfectly still.

It wasn't stopping! Leesu could not believe his eyes. He tensed his muscles and suddenly sprang from the tree line. Leesu caught the rabbit in three leaps.

How did this happen? he wondered. Then looking down, he knew. The ground was covered in a white coat as snowy as his own. The rabbit had not seen him.

Leesu howled and barked with joy, picking up mouthfuls of snow and throwing them into the air. Perhaps he could survive after all!

Weeks passed, and Leesu learned that the white coat that had shamed him in the summer now saved him. He could hide from even the sharpest rabbit.

And one day he found his size an advantage as well. He went to drink at the stream only to discover that the water was hard. When he tried to lick it, it stuck to his tongue. Leesu saw running water further out and took a tentative step onto the hard water.

The wind blew from his right and he smelled a familiar scent. It was his sister, Eele. He turned his head and saw her downriver, walking out on the hard water. Suddenly, there was a sharp crack, the hard water broke, and Eele fell through!

Leesu ran as fast as his short legs would carry him along the shore to where his sister was yelping and trying to crawl out of the icy water. Her weight was too great, and the edge of the hard water cracked each time she tried to pull herself up. Leesu walked gingerly out to the hole and reached forward, grabbing Eele by the fur at the back of her neck and pulling. Though the hard water made crackling sounds, it did not break under Leesu's much lighter weight. Soon he had pulled Eele shivering to the shore.

Eele was very thin, even thinner than Leesu had been when he left the pack. She told him the pack had come on hard times, and there was very little to eat. The game could see their dark coats against the snow, and the hard water was so thin at the edges that they broke through before they could fish. Leesu walked back out across the hard water and found he could stand right on the edge of the hole and fish. He was so light the hard water didn't break. He brought several fish for Eele to eat and even managed to catch a rabbit.

The next day, Leesu squeezed his small frame down the rabbit hole again. He took the rabbit he caught to his family's den to share and followed up with two mice and another rabbit. Throughout the winter, the little white wolf continued to hunt and provide for his family and the pack. His size and color ensured the pack's survival through those long cold months.

In the spring, his brothers and sisters laughed with Leesu, not at him, and the pack learned that even the smallest one or the one who is different has a place in nature's plan.

About the Author

Lee Allen is a graduate of Capital University, Texas Christian University, and the Air War College. He is a retired officer and began teaching elementary school in Roy, Utah, in 1993. He and his wife, Susan, have been married fifty-one years and are the servants to six cats and a dog. He became interested in storytelling as a child by listening to his great-grandmother at bedtime.

About the Book

The Little White Wolf is the story of Leesu, born smaller than his siblings and different in color. The wolf pack laughs at him and rejects him. But nature has a place for all of us, and Leesu learns how to use his differences to succeed and help others.

www.ingramcontent.com/pod-product-compliance
Lightning Source LLC
Chambersburg PA
CBHW050753110526
44592CB00002B/49